BASICAL
New Ways with Beans, Pulses a...

Daphne Metland

The Boots Company Plc Nottingham England

Published on behalf of
The Boots Company PLC, Nottingham, England
by W. Foulsham & Company Limited,
Yeovil Road, Slough, Berkshire, SL1 4JH

ISBN 0–572–01341–8

Photoset in Great Britain by
Sprint Productions Ltd.
and printed in Spain by Cayfosa, Barcelona
Dep. Leg. B. 28799/85

CONTENTS

INTRODUCTION

Definition of pulses – as staple foods – nutritional value – variety available – uses to which they can be put

Peas, beans and lentils are all described as pulses. They are the seeds of plants with a bivalved pod, and are members of the leguminosae family. They have nitrogen fixing nodules on the roots which makes them very valuable to farmers as they help keep the soil in good condition and can be planted instead of leaving a field fallow for a year.

Unlike many plant products they are high in protein and are a very important food in cultures that are mainly vegetarian through choice, religion or simply lack of alternatives.

They were among the first crops to be cultivated once mankind stopped his nomadic ways and began to till the earth. Remains of peas have been found at many archaeological sites throughout the world and are mentioned in the Bible. The ancient Egyptians ate beans and used them as a symbol of life. This is highly appropriate, since other sources of protein must have been pretty scarce, and a good crop of beans may well have meant the difference between plenty and starvation. Beans were used by the ancient Greeks when casting votes — another indicator of how central they were to the life of the people. Indeed, even now in many parts of the world pulses are a staple diet with other foods added to them only occasionally.

They are grown in many parts of the world, including Europe, Asia, America and the East. It is not surprising that primitive man made the effort to cultivate this particular family of plants. Protein foods must have been scarce and it was almost impossible to preserve meats and dairy produce for long periods. Peas, beans and lentils are reasonably easy to grow, and could be dried in the sun for long term storage until next year's crop was ready. This also made them easy to transport, so they were ideal for traders to take on long journeys, both to eat on the way and to sell once they reached their destination.

In culinary terms they must have provided much needed variety in the diet. The fact that they can be served hot or cold, in stews, sauces, casseroles, mashed into pâtés or dips, combined into stuffings and rissoles or included in soups and salads, shows why they are still a popular food several thousands of years later.

They are obviously a versatile food and can be adapted to the cooking methods and culinary habits of each country in which they are grown and used. Even within each country beans, peas and lentils will be used differently by different groups. For strict vegans and vegetarians, beans supply a valuable source of protein in the diet along with minerals and dietary fibre. For anyone who eats meat they provide a good alternative dish or can be used to stretch the meat and make a tight budget go further. Dried beans can be soaked and then allowed to sprout, so supplying a fresh vegetable at any time of the year. They are then a valuable source of vitamin C, and add a fresh flavour to the diet.

Dried beans and peas are easy to find in the shops. Many large supermarkets sell the most popular beans, such as kidney beans, butter beans and haricot beans along with dried chick peas and lentils. Canned beans are a very useful standby, although they are usually more expensive. For the more unusual beans, health food shops and the very large supermarkets are the best place to try. Here you will usually find black eyed beans, the pretty pale green flageolets, shiny black beans, tiny brick-red aduki beans and lovely dark green mung beans normally used for sprouting. Asian grocers and shops specializing in Chinese foods are also good sources of pulses. Look out for green lentils as they are not easy to find but are very delicious, and for chana dal which look like tiny split peas and are sold in Indian grocers.

Since the dried versions keep so well and are not usually very expensive, it is always worth buying a small quantity of the more unusual ones whenever you see them. Beans, and lentils and peas, can add so much to the family's diet that it is worth experimenting with new dishes. Try adding a few beans to shepherd's pie or a casserole; mix a lentil purée into mashed carrots to serve with Sunday lunch; or make a quick and nutritious dip with chick peas or butter beans to serve with drinks. Beans are far from basic in their uses in the diet, and a whole new range of dishes may well become firm family favourites.

CHAPTER 1

BEANS, PEAS AND LENTILS – THE HISTORY

Simplicity of cooking – worldwide usage – value as cheap source of protein

Beans and peas, once dried, need long slow cooking, and this is ideal in agricultural communities where the fire or open range is always burning. Making a casserole that can cook all day, virtually unattended, must have suited farmers' wives busy with their chickens and pigs, or peasants out hoeing the crops.

Given that the basic cooking method is so convenient it is amazing how very different pulse-based dishes can be. No other one food appears in so many different cultures in so many different ways. Lentils are used in Britain to make a warming winter soup, while in India they appear as a spicy, creamy sauce to be served with vegetables and meats. Chick peas are used in the Middle East to produce hummus which is a garlicky dip for bread, while in Spain they go into a casserole with spicy sausages and hot peppers. In Cuba peas and black beans are mixed into a casserole that rejoices in the lovely name of 'Moors and Christians', reflecting the contrasting colours of the dish, and in China the same black beans are chopped finely and put into a gingery sauce to pour over vegetables.

In China beans are sprouted and used in stir fried dishes as well as a filling for the popular 'spring roll'. Sprouting the beans adds texture and valuable vitamins to the diet that might otherwise be lacking. Tofu is a soft cheese-like mixture made from soya beans that can also be dried and preserved. It mixes well with sweet or savoury dishes, picking up and enhancing their flavours, and is used in soups, meat dishes and as a salad dressing. Soya flour is another soya bean product widely used in the East, and these beans can even be used to make a milk, for drinking and cooking as well.

Warming soups must have been a useful way to keep out

the cold long before any form of central heating. In Germany they use lentils to produce filling earthy soups. In middle Europe they mix peas with spicy sausages in soups, and in Britain we make a curried chicken soup, and a thick pea and ham soup using a left-over knuckle bone.

The greatest contrast is possibly provided by Moog Dal pancakes made from split peas in India, the same basic ingredient that we use for pease pudding. We have been making pease pudding for many years, and Edward VII enjoyed a slice of pease pudding alongside his roast beef. It was obviously not universally popular, as the old nursery rhyme suggests:

> Pease pudding hot,
> Pease pudding cold,
> Pease pudding in the pot
> Nine days old.

It certainly reflects the importance of pulses, and indeed the monotony of the diets of many people in the middle ages!

The dishes that are handed down through history are the ones that work and are popular, despite some unknown child's complaints about pease pudding! The Indians found long ago that cooking pulses with certain spices, notably ginger and turmeric, improved the flavour and made them easier to digest. Perhaps the same reasoning is behind the wide use of ingredients such as chillis, and spicy sausages alongside pulses.

In most agricultural societies pulses still play a very important part in the diet. In the West we have tended to replace them with other foods and forget the traditional dishes. As meat became cheaper and more plentiful, and as methods of preserving improved, so pulses were scorned and left out of the diet. Beans were considered 'windy meat' and generally looked down upon, as is reflected in part of G. K. Chesterton's poem 'The Englishman':

> But he stood for England
> And knew what England means
> Unless you give him bacon
> You must not give him beans.

This often happens with many foods as a culture changes; traditional dishes are thought of as peasant food and replaced with new dishes and new foods. Their importance should not be underestimated though. In many parts of the world pulses are the main food that prevents starvation. They have been important to us in the past, and with changing views on our dietary needs peas, beans and pulses are gaining in popularity again. They have passed into our culture and language in many forms: 'spill the beans', 'alike as two peas in a pod', 'how many beans make five', and so on. In the future they are likely to make equally great impact on our diets.

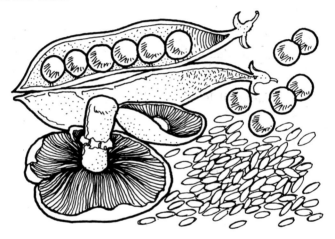

CHAPTER 2

NUTRITIONAL UPDATE

Dietary changes – usefulness of pulses – proteins, why we need them – pulses as a protein source – vitamins and minerals from pulses – calories and dietary fibre from pulses as a group

'You are what you eat' is a wise saying. Over recent years our Western diet has been shown to be a contributing factor in more and more illnesses. Over-refined foods, processed foods and too much fat and sugar have all been pointed to as detrimental to health. Additives are now being looked at more closely as possible sources of allergy, especially in children.

On a more general level it is realistic to be as fit and healthy as possible to enjoy life to the full, and to be best able to cope with any infections that may come our way. A healthy diet can go a long way towards this aim. The latest recommendations suggest that we should halve our fat and sugar intake, and increase the amount of fibre in our diet. The simplest way of doing this is to gradually move towards a diet based on unprocessed wholefoods, including more fresh vegetables and fruits, and less processed baked goods, and less meat and meat products.

Many families would rebel if faced with an overnight change in their eating habits. A gradual introduction of new dishes and small changes in established ones make life easier. Try using skimmed milk for cooking, and mixing wholemeal and plain flours for baking at first.

This is where pulses can be useful. Low in fat, high in protein and in dietary fibre, they are a natural food, unprocessed and unrefined. Include them alongside meat, or replace the occasional meat meal with pulses and they will be an exciting addition to the family's regular menu, while going a long way to help the overall improvement in the diet.

PROTEIN

Protein is an essential part of our diet. We need it for growth, for tissue repair and for the production of hormones and normal functioning of our bodies. Some groups need higher amounts of protein than others, for instance children who are growing fast, and for mothers during pregnancy and while breastfeeding. After illnesses, both major and minor, the need for protein increases. We tend to think of protein foods as being meat, fish and poultry but in fact many foods contain some protein. The type and amount varies considerably though. Potatoes, pasta and rice all have small amounts of protein in them, but we do not generally think of them as protein foods because the levels are quite low. However they do contribute to the total daily intake of protein so should not be forgotten. The type of protein foods contain varies too. Some proteins are more useful to the body than others.

Protein are made up amino acids. Some of these are essential to our diets, as they cannot be made within our bodies. Foods containing all the essential amino acids are often called complete proteins. Those foods lacking in one or more essential amino acid are referred to as incomplete proteins. So meat, dairy products, eggs, fish and poultry are protein foods, and generally thought of as such because they contain all the essential amino acids. So too do nuts and pulses, and they can be used to replace other protein foods in the diet, which is just what vegetarians, who eat no meat or fish, do. Vegans eat no meat and no animal products at all, so avoid milk, eggs, cheese etc. as well. For them, pulses and nuts are the major source of protein.

Cereals and vegetables and similar foods are incomplete proteins lacking in one or more of those essential amino acids, but that does not mean that they are useless as a protein food. The ratio of amino acids in each food varies. Indeed it is that very variation that makes beef into beef and not pork. If the level of one particular amino acid is very much lower than the levels of the other amino acids, it will prevent the body using all of the amino acids in the food. This is called the limiting amino acid. So however much of the other amino acids there are to spare only a percentage of the food can be used by the body.

However, by combining two or more foods at one meal

the small amount of one amino acid in one food can be made up by high amounts of that same amino acid in another food. This is one good reason for eating a mixture of foods at one time, along with the fact that foods generally taste better this way. We tend to eat milk with cereals, bread with cheese and so on. Pulses benefit from this mixing of foods as well and we do it without thinking about the nutritional aspects. We eat beans on toast, a wholemeal roll with our pea soup, peas and rice together in a risotto and so on. In Indian cuisine it is customary to serve a buttermilk drink with little pancakes made from split peas for breakfast, or yoghurt with a lentil curry.

The end result is that complete meals of this kind are more nutritious than meals consisting of just one food, and it is always worth including a wheat-based food such as bread, or some form of dairy product, or rice when serving pulses.

In the West we tend to think of meat as essential in our diet. Only in recent years as more people become interested in vegetarian cooking has meat begun to be eaten less often. Even if you do not want to omit meat from your family's diet it is recommended that less of the red meats are eaten and more poultry and fish are included, since they are lower in fats than beef, lamb and pork.

In many ways our need for protein is over emphasised. Quite small amounts are needed by healthy adults – around 55g (less than 2oz). No one food is all protein of course but the average diet will readily encompass this amount. Pulses, as a complete protein make a good alternative to meat products to supply the daily intake. It is tempting to think that large quantities of pulses need to be eaten but this is not so. Peas, beans and lentils supply about 10g ($\frac{1}{3}$oz) of protein in each average serving. Allowing 50g (2oz) of the dried food per person gives 100g (4oz) of the cooked food. The actual amounts of protein in the various pulses vary only slightly. Lentils have 7g per 100g portion, soya beans 9g, aduki beans and chick peas about 10g and black beans have 11g. Peas are higher in protein supplying about 12g when fresh and twice that amount when eaten as split peas. Compare this to a large egg which will give about 6.5g of protein, or 300ml ($\frac{1}{2}$ pint) of whole milk which supplies about 9g. Skimmed milk has more protein at around 14g per 300ml ($\frac{1}{2}$ pint); cottage cheese offers about 13g in every 50g (2oz); cheddar cheese has around 7g of protein in each 25g (1oz); 75g of chicken will give around 12g of protein; and a 150g (6oz) steak will give about 24g of protein.

In practise it is easy to think in terms of an average portion of beans supplying slightly more protein than one large egg, about as much protein as 300ml ($\frac{1}{2}$ pint) of whole milk, or 40g ($1\frac{1}{2}$oz) of cheese and slightly less protein than a small portion of chicken.

VITAMINS AND MINERALS

There are around 20 vitamins and minerals that are essential to our diet, but generally they are needed in quite small quantities and a wide ranging diet is likely to include all of them. Lack of any particular vitamin or mineral will eventually lead to ill health and the most well known cases are scurvy, caused by lack of vitamin C, and rickets, caused by lack of vitamin D. Pulses, as part of a well balanced diet, can make useful contributions to the vitamin and mineral levels in the diet.

Vitamin C is easily destroyed by cooking and by drying so it is really only present in useful amounts in fresh beans and peas and in beansprouts. Dried peas, lentils and beans contain small amounts of pantothenic acid and niacin and fresh peas and beans also have a little biotin. However, they are not a major dietary source of these vitamins and the diet should include plenty of fresh green vegetables as well. Most of the rest of the B group vitamins are not to be found in pulses but will be included in a wide ranging wholefood diet.

Peas supply vitamin A in quite large amounts, an average portion giving about a third of the daily needs. They also have significant amounts of potassium, giving about one sixth of daily needs. Pinto beans are the best source of potassium with a 100g (4oz) portion supplying almost all the daily needs. Kidney beans, soya beans and chick peas are also good sources. Phosphorus is available in useful quantities in most beans, particularly in black beans and lentils.

Lentils, chick peas and black beans are a good source of

iron in the diet supplying up to three quarters of the daily needs, which is why lentil soup was often served to nursing mothers and invalids.

CALORIES

> There was an old person of Dean
> Who dined on one pea and one bean;
> For he said, 'More than that,
> Would make me too fat',
> That cautious old person of Dean.

Many people assume that beans are fattening, as Edward Lear's poem would suggest. However, it is not simply a question of how many calories there are in pulses. We obtain calories either from carbohydrates, or from fats. Fats are the most concentrated source. Current recommendations suggest we should be cutting down the amount of fat we eat, particularly animal fats and increasing the amount of unrefined carbohydrates in our diet. Pulses fit into this healthy diet pattern well, since they are very low in fat, but do supply a high ratio of dietary fibre.

Split peas are the highest in calorific content of all the pulses, at around 350 calories in a 100g portion. They contain about 90 grams of carbohydrate and contribute 1.2g of dietary fibre. Fresh peas, on the other hand have only about 75 calories in each 100g and just 14g of carbohydrate. They are however high in fibre because they still have the skin of the pea, which is the major source of fibre so the fresh variety have 2g of fibre for each 100g of peas.

Soya beans, kidney beans, black eyed beans and lentils all supply around 100–110 calories in each 100g portion, and have between 1.2 and 1.5g of dietary fibre. Soya beans have the lowest amount of carbohydrate at 10g per 100g, the others all having 18–19g per 100g. Chick peas have a higher calorific value of 180 calories per 100g, with 30g of carbohydrate and 2.5g of fibre.

In practise the calorific value of pulses is lower than most protein foods simply because they contain so little fat. Compare the values of between 100 and 180 calories per 100g for pulses with that of the same amount of cheese which has around 440 calories, or with steak which has 400 calories. Even eggs have some fat in them, hence the calorific value of around 140 calories per 100g. None of these foods have any dietary fibre either, so replacing some meat dishes in the diet with ones based on pulses can go a long way to improving the diet; cutting fat, and sometimes calories and increasing fibre.

The versatility of pulses ensures that they can form an integral part of a wholefood diet, mixing well with salads, or making creamy sauces without using any fats or refined flours. Even casseroles and dips and pâtés can be made with few fatty ingredients.

A dish as simple as a vegetable dal, made with lentils and fresh vegetables, will be high in protein and many vitamins, low in fat and be a good source of dietary fibre, iron and potassium. It will also be inexpensive, an important factor to take into account when feeding a family on a fixed budget.

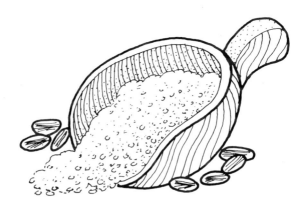

CHAPTER 3

BEANS

General guidelines on selecting beans – preparing beans – cooking beans – how to soak beans – pressure cooking – slow cooking types of beans – their uses and cooking times.

Beans are available dried or in some cases canned. Many supermarkets sell the more popular beans such as kidney beans, butter beans and haricot beans, but you may have to go to a health food shop for the more unusual ones such as black eyed beans, flageolet beans and black beans. Lima beans are very hard to find and you may well be offered butter beans instead. They are similar in shape although Lima beans are smaller with a sweeter taste.

Ideally buy beans from a shop with a good turnover, as they can become very tough if stored for many months and no amount of cooking will tenderize them. For this same reason buy little and often so that you do not have bags of beans sitting in the larder for months. The amount of grit and broken bean in amongst them varies too, so once you have found a good shop that sells a wide range of beans it is worth paying an extra penny or two a pound for good quality beans.

Pick through dried beans carefully after weighing them out. Remove any grit or small stones, and also take out any broken beans. Rinse them well to remove any dust and then soak them. All beans benefit from soaking well before cooking. Ideally they need at least six hours. The most convenient way is to soak them overnight. Since beans swell during soaking it is important to place them in a large container, and cover them with plenty of water. Do not add salt or bicarbonate of soda during soaking or cooking as these can make them tough and affect the vitamin content of the beans. Once soaked, drain the beans and then rinse well. This helps wash off the surface starch that can contribute to the unfortunate side effect of flatulence that beans can have on some people.

It is possible to speed up the soaking time if necessary.

The short soaking method involves washing the beans well, then place them in a large pan with plenty of cold water. Bring to the boil, boil for five minutes, then cover with a lid and leave to stand, off the heat, for one hour. Then drain the beans, rinse well with plenty of cold water and cook as usual. Short soaking needs more attention but is useful if you decide to cook a dish and do not have time for a long soak.

The beans can then be cooked. The usual method is to cook the beans in boiling water until tender. To do this choose a large pan and allow 750ml ($1\frac{1}{4}$ pints) of cold water to each 225g (8oz) of beans. Bring them to the boil, reduce the heat and then simmer. Kidney beans should be boiled for five to ten minutes before reducing the heat to prevent the formation of toxins which can cause a form of food poisoning.

For dishes that are to be cooked in the oven, the beans should be partly boiled, and then added to the dish to minimize the cooking time in the oven. For other dishes where beans will have little or no further cooking, they must be cooked until tender. Cooking time, in fact, varies according to how old the beans are, but a guide time is given with the detailed description of each bean.

Canned beans need no cooking and can simply be rinsed and then served as they are, or added to hot dishes and cooked for a few minutes. Remember that dried beans increase in weight during soaking, so 100g (4oz) of dried beans will be 225g (8oz) of soaked beans. So if a recipe calls for dried beans and you plan to replace them with canned ones allow twice the weight stated in the recipe.

Beans may be cooked in a pressure cooker, which will speed up the cooking to about one third of the time boiling takes. Ensure that the cooker is not overloaded, as beans can rise up during cooking. Check in the instruction book supplied with your pressure cooker. Timing will vary, so it may be necessary to depressurize the cooker and check how tender the beans are and then repressurize the cooker if necessary.

Slow cookers can also be used, but it is advisable to pre-cook the beans for ten minutes or so to speed up the cooking. Kidney beans must be pre-boiled for ten minutes before cooking in a slow cooker. Arrange the beans on the base of the slow cooker, then put the other ingredients on top. Stir well just before serving.

A GUIDE TO BEANS

Aduki Beans

This is the Japanese name for these small round reddy coloured beans. They are also known as adzuki beans and in Indian cookery they are called Ma. They have an almost sweet taste, and are often used for making vegetarian burgers. Their pinky red colour is used in some Oriental cookery to combine with rice, since pink is considered a lucky colour. They are generally available dried in health food shops.

Soaking: overnight, or use short soak method.
Cooking time: about 30 minutes.

Black Beans

These are a variety of kidney bean and are a bright shiny black colour. The inside is grey and they have a tasty almost nutty texture. They can be used instead of kidney beans in many dishes. Traditional uses include black bean sauce in Chinese cookery and in a Cuban dish called Moors and Christians where they are mixed with rice, and sometimes peas. Mostly available dried in health food shops, but can also be bought salted from Chinese shops.

Soaking: overnight, or use the short soak method.
Cooking time: about 1 hour.

Black Eyed Beans

These creamy white beans have a black spot on each of them. They come mainly from America and were once a staple dish in southern parts of the country. They hold their shape well and are useful to use in casseroles and vegetable dishes. They can be used in place of haricot beans or butter beans.

Soaking: overnight, or use the short soak method.
Cooking time: 40–50 minutes.

Bortlotti Beans

These are available canned or dried. A member of the

kidney bean family, they are slightly speckled in appearance and are very attractive to add to salads. Their texture makes them a good addition to soups as well.

Soaking: overnight or use the short soak method.
Cooking time: $1-1\frac{1}{4}$ hours.

Butter Beans

Butter beans are sometimes called calico beans. They are large white kidney shaped beans and are easily available dried or canned. They are excellent in salads and as a vegetable, but do tend to go mushy during cooking, so take care to check frequently to catch them while tender but whole. Small cans are a useful addition to the store cupboard as a base for an instant salad, or to use to make a dip to serve with vegetable sticks.

Soaking: overnight, or use the short soak method.
Cooking time: $1\frac{1}{4}$ hours.

Broad Beans

One of the few beans that grow in Britain, broad beans are in season for a few weeks in early summer. They are also available frozen, canned and dried. They are flat and rounded in shape with a tough outer skin. Useful as a vegetable and in casseroles. Also known as Fava beans or Windsor beans. Dried broad beans need overnight soaking, or use the short soak method.

Cooking time: $1\frac{1}{2}$ hours.

Flageolet Beans

These small pale green beans are very delicious. They have a delicate flavour and hold their shape well so they are excellent in salads and blend well with fish and poultry. Mostly available dried in health food shops, their name comes from the French for flute. Rather expensive compared to other beans, and often hard to track down, but well worth the effort.

Soaking: overnight, or use the short soak method.
Cooking time: $1\frac{1}{2}$ hours.

Haricot Beans

The ubiquitous baked bean by any other name! Widely available either canned or dried this is a white rounded bean with a soft smooth texture. It cooks well and holds its shape during cooking so is often used in stews and casseroles.

Soaking: overnight, or use the short soak method.
Cooking time: $1\frac{1}{2}$ hours

Lima Beans
Similar in shape to butter beans but smaller and sweeter. They are hard to find even in health food shops. Butter beans make a good alternative, but the Lima bean is useful in salads where the flavour of the bean comes through more.

Soaking: overnight, or use the short soak method.
Cooking time: 1 hour.

Kidney Beans
Widely used and very popular in many kinds of cooking these are kidney shaped and a lovely glossy deep red colour. They are available canned or dried, and used in dishes such as chilli con carne, as well as in sauces, as a vegetable and in salads. The kidney bean was originally grown in America and only introduced to Europe when America was first explored. In bean history this is a new bean for European cookery. Its fine texture and almost meaty taste make it popular.

Soaking: overnight, or use the short soak method.
Cooking time: 1 hour.

Mung Beans
Mung beans are tiny dark green beans, available mostly from health food shops. Not often cooked as a bean, but generally used for sprouting. The whole bean can be cooked and eaten, and since they are so small and have quite a sweet taste they can be cooked without soaking. They are ideal as a sprouting bean as they take only two to three days to produce good crisp sprouts, which are small and tender.

Sprouting beans is simple to do and good fun for children to try. Wash the mung beans, soak them overnight in cold water and then rinse them well. Place in a large jam jar. Remember that they increase in bulk up to ten times their original size, so choose a large jar. Cover the top of the jar with a piece of muslin, or use a disposable kitchen cloth –

the type with fine holes are ideal. Keep in a dark cupboard and rinse with water two to three times a day. It is often easier to keep the jar in the kitchen so that you remember to rinse the sprouts. In this case either place it in a shoe box, or wrap some thick brown paper around the jar to keep the light out. To rinse them allow the cold water to run through the muslin or kitchen cloth, swill it round and then tip the water out. Prop the jar on the draining board for a few minutes to allow the last of the water to run out.

After two or three days the beans will have grown long white sprouts. When you want to use them, take the cloth off the jar, tip the beans into a large colander and rinse them well. You can discard the little green cases left behind from the original beans, although some people do eat these.

Once sprouted beans only keep for a couple of days before going brown, so it is wise to start another batch straight away, so you always have some fresh sprouts to hand. This method has the advantage of being quick and easy to do and producing very cheap beansprouts. They are available in supermarkets both fresh and canned but are very much more expensive. Other beans such as soya can be used for sprouting, but grow a bigger sprout.

Soya Beans

Rather unattractive in appearance while dry, soya beans have been known and widely used in the East for thousands of years. They are small, rather knobbly brown beans, and they have the highest amount of protein of any of the pulses. They can be ground into a flour and soya flour can easily be added to many baked dishes to improve their protein content. Try adding soya flour to shortbread for a nutty texture and finer flavour. It can be used in cakes too and to make a smooth 'soya cream'. Soya milk can be made from soya flour and a type of 'cheese' for vegetarians.

The beans themselves are available dried and canned. They take quite a long time to tenderize while cooking so it is generally worthwhile to cook a batch and freeze the cooked beans.

Soya beans are used to make soya bean curd, which is rather like soft cheese. It is tasteless but picks up the flavour of other foods it is combined with so is a useful way of improving the protein content of many dishes. It can be used with sweet or savoury dishes, added to soups, stirred into a meat dish, combined with yoghurt to make a dessert or as a base for a salad dressing. Called tofu, it is sold in health food shops, and sometimes is available dried in Chinese shops. Now available in a long life form, like milk in cartons, so can be safely stored in the fridge for several months. The beans can be used in curries, casseroles and salads.

Soaking: overnight, or use the short soak method.
Cooking time: 4 hours.

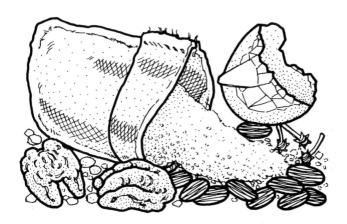

CHAPTER 4

PEAS

General guidelines on selecting peas – preparing peas – cooking peas – how to soak peas – uses and cooking times

Fresh peas are really only in season for six weeks or so, and fresh peas served with lamb for Sunday lunch is a real sign that spring is here. For the rest of the year we have to eat frozen, canned or dried peas instead. In summer mange tout are available. These are very young tender peas in the pod, and the whole vegetable can be cooked and eaten, hence the name – 'eat all'. They are excellent steamed and served with a little butter, or can be used in stir fried dishes.

Chick Peas

These are small, round light brown peas, also known as Garbanzos. They are available dried or canned and make excellent salads and lovely creamy dips like hummus. They are also good curried as their meaty texture holds up well during cooking and their bland, almost creamy taste combines well with spices. They are served in India as a hot spicy snack food. Once cooked they can be stored in the fridge for 2–3 days. They may also be frozen and thawing may be speeded up by tipping them into a colander and allowing it to stand under running cold water. It is worth keeping a can of these in the store cupboard for quick meals as well as buying them dried. Quite widely available.
Soaking: long or short soak.
Cooking time: 1-1½ hours.

Dried Whole Peas

Available dried or canned. They look rather like wizened versions of fresh peas and once soaked and cooked have a good flavour and hold their shape quite well. Good to combine with rice in rissotto-like dishes, and also excellent for soups, giving a lovely green colour to them.
Soaking: long or short soak.
Cooking time: boil for 10 minutes, then reduce to simmer for 1½ hours.

Split Peas

Available as green split peas or more commonly yellow split peas. A special variety of pea is grown for drying. The tough outer seedpod comes off during the drying process and the pea splits in half, which makes it quicker to cook. They cook quite quickly but do not hold their shape very well. Ideal for purées, and for adding to rissoles etc. They are the main ingredient of pease pudding, giving it its bright yellow colour. Pease pudding was originally cooked in a cloth. The mixture was turned into a piece of muslin and the sides gathered round and tied to make a ball shape. It would be hung in the pot to cook while other foods were being stewed. Cut into slices it could be served hot or cold, and the cold left-overs were often fried as a supper dish. Ideal with roast meats or good just on its own. Can be cooked in a pressure cooker but peas do tend to rise up during cooking so avoid overloading the cooker and add just a little cooking oil to the water – 1 tablespoon is usually enough.

To make a split pea purée use 225g (8oz) split peas to 600ml (1 pint) water. Soak and rinse well. Place in a large pan with the water, bring to the boil and boil for five minutes. Reduce the heat and simmer for 45 to 50 minutes until all the water is absorbed and the peas are soft. They can then be beaten with a wooden spoon or puréed in a processor or blender. Take care to check during the cooking time that the water has not boiled away and to stir the pan occasionally. Once cooked, the split peas or the purée will keep for two to three days in the 'fridge, or can be frozen for four to five months. Thaw completely before use. Split peas are widely available dried and pease pudding is also available in cans. They can be used as a substitute for chana dal in Indian cookery. This is similar in colour but the grains are much smaller. It is used in sauces and in making little pancakes, often served for breakfast.

Soaking: long or short soak.

Cooking time: 30-40 minutes.

CHAPTER 5

LENTILS

General guidelines on selecting lentils – preparing lentils – cooking lentils – their uses and cooking times

Lentils are the seeds of the plant lens asulenta. They are particularly high in iron and phosphorus and traditionally lentil soup was fed to invalids and nursing mothers. It is very comforting to eat lentil soup when recovering from colds or 'flu. When the structure of the eye was investigated the lens was so called because it resembled the shape of the lentil seed. Lentils are widely grown and used throughout the world and are generally available either as red lentils or green lentils.

Red Lentils
Also sometimes called Egyptian lentils. They are the lovely bright orangey-red ones that are sold in supermarkets and health food shops. They do not need soaking, but should be washed and rinsed before cooking. They cook quickly and easily turn into a pulp. They are used in Indian cookery to make spicy, nutritious sauces, or served as a vegetable. They can also be served as a purée, or mixed with other vegetables such as mashed potatoes, or carrot or turnip, or combined with other vegetables to make rissoles.

Red lentils make an ideal baby food as they cook so quickly and can simply be beaten to a pulp with a wooden spoon. Add a little grated cheese or cooked carrot for variety. Lentils also make a good quick curry and combine well with tomatoes to make a sauce to serve with pasta. They are a good standby food since they need no soaking and once cooked can be stored in the fridge for two days. The purée freezes well, but thaw completely at room temperature before reheating.

To make a lentil purée mix 225g (8oz) lentils with 400ml ($\frac{3}{4}$ pint) of cold water in a pan. Bring to the boil, then reduce the heat and simmer gently for about 30 minutes until all the water has been absorbed. Check from time to time that the heat is not too fierce, and stir once or twice to help prevent

them sticking. Beat well with a wooden spoon, or purée in a blender or processor.
Soaking: none needed.
Cooking: 30 minutes.

Continental Lentils

These are deep green or sometimes browny-yellow. Often they are called German lentils, not because they are grown there, but rather because they are the type often used in German cookery. Their flavour is finer than that of red lentils, and they retain their shape once cooked so are useful in salads and other dishes where whole lentils are needed. Excellent curried, or to mix with other vegetables. Used in soups to give body as well as for their high protein value. In Indian cookery they are often mixed with spinach and cream cheese. Store cooked lentils in the fridge for 2 – 3 days, or freeze. Thaw completely before use.

To cook continental lentils, place 225g (8oz) lentils in a pan with 400ml ($\frac{3}{4}$ pint) cold water. Bring to the boil, reduce heat and simmer gently for 30–40 minutes until tender but whole.
Soaking: none needed.
Cooking: 30–40 minutes.

CHAPTER 6

RECIPES

PEA AND BACON SOUP

Serves 4

225g (8oz) peas, dried
100g (4oz) bacon, streaky
25g (1oz) butter
1 clove garlic

1 litre (1¾ pints) vegetable
   stock
Freshly ground black
   pepper
1 teaspoon mint, dried

1 Soak peas overnight, drain and rinse well.

2 Chop the bacon finely, and fry in the butter until crisp. Remove the bacon, put to one side. Crush the garlic and fry in the butter until brown. Add the peas, stock, pepper and mint.

3   Bring to the boil, then simmer for $1-1\frac{1}{2}$ hours until tender. Liquidize. Return to the pan and heat gently.

4   Serve sprinkled with bacon pieces.

Note: Freeze for up to 4 months.

CHILLI CON CARNE

Serves 4

2-3 green chillies
2 tablespoons vegetable oil
$\frac{1}{2}$ teaspoon cayenne pepper
500g ($1\frac{1}{4}$lb) minced beef
600ml (1 pint) beef stock
400g (14oz) tomatoes, canned

225g (8oz) kidney beans, soaked and rinsed
2 tablespoons tomato purée
Few drops Worcestershire sauce

1   Chop the chillies and cook, with the seeds, in the oil. Add the cayenne pepper, stir well, and then stir in the beef and cook until lightly browned. Add the stock, tomatoes, kidney beans, tomato purée and Worcestershire sauce. Stir all well and bring to the boil.

2   Allow to boil for 10 minutes, then reduce heat to simmer and cook partly covered for $1\frac{1}{2} - 2$ hours. Stir occasionally during this time. If the mixture becomes a little dry add 150ml ($\frac{1}{4}$ pint) extra stock.

3   Serve hot with toast or hot pitta bread.

HUMMUS
Serves 4

430g (15oz) chick peas, canned
1 clove garlic
Sea salt and freshly ground black pepper to taste

2 tablespoons good salad oil
1 tablespoon lemon juice
1 tablespoon tahini

1 Place the chick peas, garlic and seasonings in a blender or processor. Blend and then add the oil, lemon juice and tahini and blend until smooth and creamy.

2 Serve as a dip with vegetable sticks and savoury biscuits.

Note: This can also be made with dried chick peas – soak, drain, rinse and cook until very tender.

FLAGEOLET AND TUNA SALAD

Serves 4

50g (2oz) flageolet beans
200g (7oz) tuna fish, canned

1-2 tablespoons wine
  vinegar
4 spring onions

1 Soak the beans, rinse, then cook until tender. Drain and rinse again.

2 Open the can of tuna, and place all the contents in a bowl. (Do not drain the oil off.) Break up the tuna meat roughly. Add the beans and the vinegar and stir gently together.

3 Chop the onions and sprinkle on top.

This mixture can also be used to stuff tomatoes and served as a starter. It will fill 4 medium tomatoes. Chill briefly before serving.

CURRIED CHICKEN AND LENTIL SOUP

Serves 4

1 large onion
1 tablespoon vegetable oil
2 teaspoons curry powder
1 tablespoon sherry
1.2 litres (2 pints) chicken
   stock
3-4 carrots

225g (8oz) cooked chicken
100g (4oz) lentils
Sea salt
Freshly ground black
   pepper

1   Chop the onion and fry in the oil until soft. Add the curry powder, and fry gently. Pour in the sherry and stir well. Add the stock, and the carrots cut into little sticks. Add the chopped chicken meat and the lentils.

2 Bring to the boil, and simmer for 15 minutes until the vegetables are tender. Season to taste.

3 Serve hot with wholemeal bread or croûtons.

Freeze for up to 3 months. Cool and pour into a freezer container. Thaw for 4 – 6 hours at room temperature and heat in a pan, stirring occasionally.

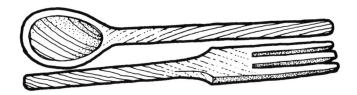

TOMATO AND LENTIL SOUP

Serves 4

1 tablespoon vegetable oil
1 clove garlic
1 onion
1 carrot, chopped
1 small potato, chopped
$\frac{1}{2}$ red pepper
400g (14oz) tomatoes, canned

100g (4oz) lentils
900ml ($1\frac{1}{2}$ pints) vegetable stock
Few drops tabasco sauce
Freshly ground black pepper
Sea salt

1 Heat the oil in a large pan. Crush the garlic, chop the onion and fry until browned. Add the carrot and potato. Thinly slice the red pepper, add to the pan and stir well.

2 Pour in the tomatoes, lentils and the stock. Stir well, bring to the boil and then simmer for 20 minutes until the vegetables are tender.

3 Purée in a blender or processor and return to the pan. Add tabasco sauce and seasonings to taste and reheat gently.

4 Serve hot with wholemeal bread or croûtons.

Note: To freeze, cool and pour into freezer container. Thaw four to six hours at room temperature and reheat in a pan, stirring occasionally.

BUTTER BEAN STUFFED EGGS

Serves 4

6 eggs
100g (4oz) can or 50g (2oz)
dried butter beans
25g (1oz) butter

Freshly ground black
pepper
2-3 drops tabasco sauce
1 bunch watercress
12 small gherkins

1   If using dried butter beans, soak, rinse and cook until tender.

2   Hardboil the eggs for 10 minutes, then cool in cold water. Mash the butter beans, or place in blender or processor and blend until smooth.

3   Shell the eggs, cut in half lengthways and remove the yolk. Reserve one yolk, and put the rest in with the

butter beans and mash or blend. Melt the butter and pour into the mixture along with plenty of pepper and the tabasco sauce. Mash together or blend. Pile the filling into the egg whites.

4   Arrange on a plate with the washed watercress in the middle. Sieve the reserved egg yolk and sprinkle a little over each egg. Make the gherkins into fans by cutting along the length of each 4 times. Spread the cut pieces open to make a fan shape and use to garnish each egg.

MIXED BEANS IN WHITE SAUCE
Serves 4

50g (2oz) peas
50g (2oz) haricot beans
50g (2oz) soya beans
50g (2oz) aduki beans

35g (1½oz) butter
35g (1½oz) wholemeal flour
300ml (½ pint) milk
2 tomatoes

1   Soak, rinse and cook the peas and beans until soft. Drain and place in an ovenproof dish.

2   Melt the butter, add the flour and cook together for 1 minute. Gradually stir in the milk, bring to the boil and cook until thickened. Season well, and pour over the beans.

3   Arrange slices of tomato on top and cook in the oven at 180°C/350°F/Gas Mark 4 for 15-20 minutes.

Note: This dish is ideal to make with leftover beans, and the type and proportions can be varied according to taste.

GREEN BEAN AND CHICKEN SALAD

100g (4oz) flageolet beans
½ lettuce
100g (4oz) beansprouts
1 avocado
225g (8oz) cooked chicken

225g (8oz) pineapple
(canned in juice)
5 tablespoons good salad oil
½ tablespoon wine vinegar
Sea salt and freshly ground
black pepper

1 Soak the flageolet beans, rinse well and then cook until
   tender.

2 Shred the lettuce and place in a salad bowl. Blanch the
   beansprouts with boiling water. Stand for 1 minute then
   rinse with cold water and drain. Cut the avocado into
   quarters, and prise the flesh away from the stone. Then
   peel the skin off. Slice along the length. Chop the

chicken. Lift the pineapple pieces out of the juice and chop them. Reserve the juice.

3   Add cooled beans, beansprouts, chicken and chopped pineapple to the lettuce. Mix 2 tablespoons of the pineapple juice with the oil, wine vinegar and seasonings to make a dressing and pour this over the salad. Mix in well.

4   Arrange the slices of avocado in circles on the top and stand for 10 minutes before serving to allow the dressing to soak in.

BACON AND BEANSPROUT PANCAKES

Makes 6-8

300ml ($\frac{1}{2}$ pint) skimmed milk	50g (2oz) mushrooms
1 egg	100g (4oz) bacon
50g (2oz) wholemeal flour	175g (6oz) beansprouts
50g (2oz) plain flour	2 tablespoons sherry
3 tablespoons vegetable oil	Few drops soy sauce
1 stick celery	

1   Mix the milk and egg together with a fork. Sieve the flours together, and make a well in the middle. Gradually beat in the milk and egg mixture until a batter is formed. Stir in 1 tablespoon of oil. Stand the mixture for 30 minutes.

2   Chop the celery, mushrooms and bacon and fry in 1 tablespoon of oil until brown. Add the beansprouts and stir well. Mix the sherry and soy sauce together and pour on top. Cook for 3 minutes.

3   Make the pancakes, using the remaining oil, and stack with a layer of greaseproof paper between each one. This mixture should make 6 large pancakes or 8 small ones.

4   Use the beansprout mixture to stuff the pancakes and fold each one into a small parcel. Place in a large shallow dish with the folded sides down. Cover with foil and bake at 200°C/400°F/Gas Mark 6 for 10 minutes.

SPRING POTATO SALAD WITH TOFU DRESSING

Serves 4-6

50g (2oz) green lentils
1 bay leaf
1 clove garlic
225g (8oz) new potatoes
3 eggs
$\frac{1}{2}$ cucumber
2 tomatoes
125g (5oz) tofu

2 teaspoons wine vinegar
1 teaspoon french mustard
$\frac{1}{2}$ teaspoon dark brown
  sugar
1 tablespoon salad oil
Sea salt and freshly ground
  black pepper to taste
1 tablespoon tarragon,
  chopped

1 Cook the lentils in water, with the bay leaf and garlic,
   until soft – about 20-30 minutes. Scrub the potatoes, cut
   into cubes and boil until tender. Hardboil the eggs. Cut

the cucumber into cubes, leaving the skin on. Cut the tomatoes into eighths.

2   Combine the cooked lentils, potatoes, cucumber and tomatoes in a large bowl.

3   Mix the tofu, vinegar, seasonings and oil together in a blender until smooth. Pour on to the salad and mix well to coat the ingredients. Arrange in a bowl, with the eggs cut into eighths around the edge.

4   Serve as a lunch with wholemeal bread or warmed pitta bread.

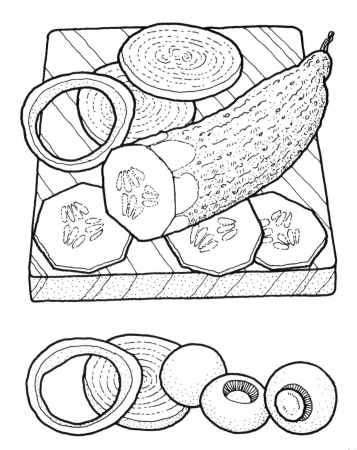

MIXED VEGETABLE SALAD

Serves 4

1 large potato
2 carrots
2 sticks celery
50g (2oz) haricot beans, cooked
50g (2oz) peas, cooked

2-3 tablespoons mayonnaise
1 teaspoon lemon juice
Sea salt and freshly ground black pepper
1 carrot

1 Cut the potato, carrots and celery into cubes or small slices. Cook together in rapidly boiling water until just tender.

2 Mix with the peas and beans and, while still warm, mix in the mayonnaise, lemon juice and seasoning.

3 Garnish with raw grated carrot.

This dish can be made with a variety of beans and is a good way of using up leftovers.

CHICK PEA CASSEROLE WITH PORK

Serves 4

1.5kg (3lbs) knuckle of pork
150ml ($\frac{1}{4}$ pint) cider
1 small onion
2 bay leaves
1 teaspoon caraway seeds
8 small carrots

$\frac{1}{2}$ an apple, peeled and
  chopped
450g (1lb) chick peas,
  canned
2 teaspoons cornflour

1 Place the pork in a large pan and add 1.2 litres (2 pints) of cold water, the cider, the onion roughly chopped, bay leaves and caraway seeds. Bring to the boil, then simmer for 40 minutes.

2 Scrape and trim carrots, cut into sticks and add to the pan. Simmer for another 40 minutes.

3 When the meat is tender, remove from the pan and cut the meat off the bone. Trim into cubes. Add another 600ml (1 pint) of water to the pan, and the apple, and the chick peas. Stir in the meat pieces and cook for 10 minutes.

4 Mix the cornflour with a little cold water until a smooth paste is formed. Add some of the stock from the pan, and then pour this mixture back into the pan, and bring to the boil to allow it to thicken.

5 Serve hot with wholemeal bread or brown rice.

CASSOULET

Serves 4

500g (1¼lb) haricot beans
175g (6oz) belly of pork

4 cloves garlic
900g (2lb) shoulder of lamb

2 tablespoons vegetable oil	400g (14oz) tomatoes, canned
6 whole peppercorns	2 teaspoons tomato purée
2 bay leaves	100g (4oz) wholemeal breadcrumbs
2 blade of mace	
5 parsley stalks	

1   Rinse the beans, soak, then rinse again. Place in a large hob or ovenproof pan.

2   Derind and chop the pork, crush the garlic cloves and add both to beans. Pour on 1.2 litres (2 pints) of cold water. Bring to the boil, cover and simmer for 1 hour.

3   Bone the lamb and cut into cubes. Fry in the oil until just brown. Add to the beans along with the herbs and spices (tie them together in a small square of butter muslin or cotton and hang from the edge of the pan).

4   Cook gently for 2 hours, adding extra water if necessary, and stirring occasionally. Then add the tomatoes, and the tomato purée, and stir well. Cook for a further hour, until the sauce is thick and creamy.

5   Sprinkle the breadcrumbs over the top of the casserole and place in the oven. Cook for 30-40 minutes at 190°C/375°F/Gas Mark 5 until brown and crisp on top.

CHICK PEA CURRY

Serves 4

1 large onion
50g (2oz) butter
2 teaspoons curry powder
1 teaspoon turmeric
Pinch of ground ginger
1 tablespoon desiccated
  coconut
225g (8oz) chick peas,
  cooked

300ml ($\frac{1}{2}$ pint) vegetable
  stock
15g ($\frac{1}{2}$oz) sultanas
1 bay leaf
1 red pepper
1 leek
Sea salt and freshly ground
  pepper

1   Slice the onion and fry in the butter until brown. Stir in
    the spices and cook.

2   Infuse the coconut in 4 tablespoons of boiling water for
    10 minutes, then strain the liquid into the pan and discard

the coconut. Add the chick peas, stock, sultanas and bay leaf to the pan. Bring to the boil, cover and simmer for 25 minutes.

3   Add the sliced leek and pepper, and cook for a further 20-30 minutes until the vegetables are tender and the sauce thick.

4   Serve hot with rice, or pitta bread.

BOSTON BAKED BEANS

Serves 4

225g (8oz) belly of pork
2 tablespoons vegetable oil
1 onion
1 clove garlic
400g (14oz) tomatoes, canned

2 teaspoons tomato purée
500g (1¼lb) haricot beans soaked and rinsed
600ml (1 pint) vegetable stock

1   Remove rind from the pork and cut into cubes. Fry lightly in the oil in a large saucepan until brown. Lift out meat with a draining spoon, and put to one side.

2   Chop the onion, crush the garlic and fry in the pan. Add the canned tomatoes and break up with a spoon. Add tomato purée, haricot beans and the pieces of meat. Stir well, and gradually stir in the stock.

3   Bring to the boil, partly cover with a lid and simmer for 30-40 minutes until the beans are tender and the sauce is thick and creamy. Serve hot.

BRAISED CHICKEN WITH BEANS

Serves 4

4 chicken portions
2 tablespoons vegetable oil
3 sticks celery, chopped

1 onion, chopped
1 teaspoon cumin seeds
1 tablespoon garam masala

900ml (1½ pints) chicken stock)
2 teaspoons cornflour
3 large carrots, chopped

2 potatoes, chopped
175g (6oz) beans and peas mixed (use canned or soaked cooked ones)

1   Brown the chicken portions in the oil, in a large oven-proof casserole. Remove, and then cook the celery and

onion in the oil. Add the cumin seeds and the garam masala and cook for 1-2 minutes.

2 Add the carrot, potato and the beans/peas. Then add the chicken portions, and pour the stock around them.

3 Cover and cook in the oven at 190°C/375°F/ Gas Mark 5 for 40-50 minutes. Thicken the stock with the cornflour 10 minutes before the end of cooking.

BLACK EYED BEANS WITH MUSHROOMS

Serves 4

225g (8oz) black eyed beans
1 clove garlic
1 tablespoon vegetable oil
1 teaspoon cumin seeds
2 chillies
$\frac{1}{2}$ teaspoon turmeric
225g (8oz) button mushrooms
450ml ($\frac{3}{4}$ pint) vegetable stock

1 Soak the beans and rinse well. Place in a pan of water, bring to the boil and then simmer for 25 minutes until tender. Rinse well.

2 Fry the crushed garlic in the oil until brown. Add the cumin seeds and fry lightly. Chop the chillies and fry until soft. Add the turmeric and stir well.

3 Wipe the mushrooms and cut any large ones into quarters. Fry with the other ingredients, stirring gently until they are brown.

4 Add the stock and the beans. Stir well, scraping the pan juices from the base and sides of the pan. Bring to the boil, then simmer for 40 minutes until the stock is absorbed. Serve hot.

KIDNEY BEAN AND VEGETABLE LASAGNE

Serves 4

225g (8oz) kidney beans
5-6 lasagne slices
50g (2oz) butter
50g (2oz) wholemeal flour
600ml (1 pint) skimmed milk
75-100g (3-4oz) strong
  cheese
1 leek
1 clove garlic
1 stick celery

50g (2oz) mushrooms
2 tablespoons vegetable oil
1 tablespoon sherry
2 tablespoons wholemeal
  flour
Few drops soy sauce
450ml ($\frac{3}{4}$ pint) vegetable
  stock
225g (8oz) courgettes

1   Soak the kidney beans and cook until tender. Cook the lasagne slices in plenty of boiling water for 10-12 minutes. Drain and rinse with cold water.

2   Melt the butter in a large pan, add the flour and cook for 1 minute. Then gradually stir in the milk. Bring to the boil, stirring. Remove from the heat and season well. Grate the cheese and add half of it to the sauce.

3   Cook the sliced leek, crushed garlic and sliced mushrooms and celery in the oil, until they are browned and soft. Add the sherry and stir well. Then stir in the flour.

4   Mix the soy sauce with the stock and gradually stir this into the flour and vegetables. Bring to the boil, add the kidney beans and simmer for 15 minutes.

5   Slice the courgettes and place on the base of an oven-proof dish. Pour half the vegetable sauce over the top. Lay half the lasagne slices on top and then pour the remaining vegetable sauce on. Cover with lasagne slices. Spread the cheese sauce on top, and sprinkle with grated cheese.

6   Bake at 190°C/375°F/Gas Mark 5 for 20-30 minutes.

TAGLIATELLE
Serves 4

1 leek
1 tablespoon vegetable oil
225g (8oz) tomatoes, canned
50g (2oz) lentils
600ml (1 pint) vegetable
  stock

1 teaspoon basil, dried
Freshly ground black
  pepper
225g (8oz) tagliatelle, dried
  or 400g (14oz) tagliatelle,
  fresh

1 Fry the chopped leek in the oil until soft. Add the tomatoes, and break them up with a spoon. Add the lentils and stock and bring to the boil. Simmer for 30-40 minutes until soft and thick. Add basil and pepper, stir well and simmer for a further 5 minutes.

2 Cook the tagliatelle in plenty of boiling water, until soft but with some 'bite'. Fresh pasta will take only 2-3 minutes; dried longer. Drain and serve with sauce.

RICE AND PEA RISOTTO

Serves 4

1 onion
½ green pepper
½ red pepper
3 medium mushrooms
1 tablespoon vegetable oil
25g (1oz) butter
½ teaspoon turmeric

1 teaspoon coriander
25g (1oz) cashew nuts
225g (8oz) brown rice
900ml (1½ pints) vegetable
  stock
100g (4oz) dried peas,
  soaked and cooked

1 Chop the onion. Deseed and slice the peppers. Wash
   and slice the mushrooms.

2 Fry the vegetables in the oil and butter, until softened.
   Add the turmeric, coriander, cashew nuts and rice and
   stir well. Add the stock and the peas.

3   Bring to the boil, then simmer with the lid on for 50-60 minutes, until the liquid is absorbed, and the rice is soft.

4   Serve hot with wholemeal or pitta bread.

ADUKI BURGERS
Makes 4

175g (6oz) aduki beans
2 carrots, grated
25g (1oz) cashew nuts, chopped
50g (2oz) wholemeal breadcrumbs

Few drops soy sauce
$\frac{1}{2}$ teaspoon yeast extract
Sea salt and freshly ground black pepper
1 egg, beaten
Vegetable oil

1   Soak and rinse the beans, then cook until tender. While still warm, mash with potato masher or place in a food processor.

49

2 Add the carrots and the cashew nuts. Mix in the bread-crumbs and seasonings and mash altogether or process for a few seconds.

3 Add enough of the egg to bind the mixture and then form into 4 burgers. Chill for 30 minutes before frying in shallow oil.

4 Serve hot with wholemeal baps and salad.

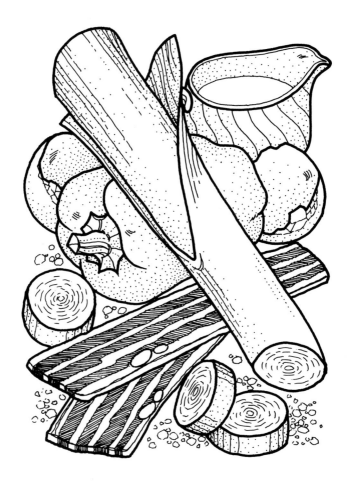

BEANSPROUTS WITH PRAWNS

Serves 4

1 leek	100g (4oz) prawns
2 tablespoons vegetable oil	225g (8oz) beansprouts
50g (2oz) mushrooms	2 tablespoons sherry
½ red pepper	Few drops soy sauce

1   Slice the leek and fry in the oil in a large shallow pan or wok. Once it is soft, slice the mushrooms and add to the pan. Fry lightly until just browned.

2   Slice the pepper thinly and fry, then add the prawns and fry until brown. Add the beansprouts and fry, stirring well for 2-3 minutes.

3   Mix the sherry with the soy sauce and pour over the ingredients in the pan. Stir well for 1 minute and then serve immediately.

VEGETABLE AND CHEESE QUICHE

Serves 4

100g (4oz) wholemeal flour
25g (1oz) lard
25g (1oz) butter
2-3 tablespoons water
1 teaspoon brown sugar
1 teaspoon vegetable oil
100g (4oz) curd cheese
2 eggs
200ml (7 fl oz) milk

Sea salt and freshly ground
  black pepper
2 teaspoons parsley,
  chopped
100g (4oz) broad beans,
  soaked and cooked until
  tender, or canned
2 tomatoes

1 Rub fats into flour until the mixture resembles fine breadcrumbs. Mix the water, brown sugar and oil together

and use to bind the pastry. Mix to a dough and then rest in the refrigerator for 30 minutes. Use to line a 20cm (8 in.) flan ring.

2   Beat the curd cheese in a large bowl until soft. Mix the eggs with the milk and season well. Add the chopped parsley, and then gradually beat this mixture into the curd cheese.

3   Place the broad beans in the base of the flan ring, and pour the cheese mixture over. Thinly slice the tomatoes and arrange on top.

4   Bake at 200°C/400°F/Gas Mark 6 for 30 minutes until brown and set.

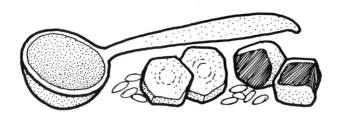

PEASE PUDDING

Serves 4

225g (8oz) yellow split peas
1 large onion
50g (2oz) butter

1 egg
Sea salt and freshly ground
   black pepper

1   Soak the peas for 30 minutes, then drain and rinse. Place in a pan with sufficient cold water to cover them. Simmer until tender. Drain.

2   Fry the chopped onion in the butter until soft but not brown. Add the peas and stir well.

3   Beat the egg, season well and stir into the pea mixture. Place in a lightly oiled casserole dish and bake at 180°C/350°F/Gas Mark 4 for 30 minutes.

4   Serve hot cut into slices with roast meats.

STUFFED MUSHROOMS

Serves 4

100g (40oz) split peas
1 carrot
1 onion
1 potato
100g (4oz) wholemeal
  breadcrumbs
1 tablespoon vegetable oil
$\frac{1}{2}$ teaspoon french mustard

$\frac{1}{2}$ teaspoon yeast extract
2 teaspoons parsley,
  chopped
1 sage leaf
1 tablespoon sherry
1 tablespoon water
6-8 open mushrooms

1 Soak the peas for 30 minutes in water. Roughly chop the carrot, onion and potato.

2 Boil the peas in fresh water until soft, drain and mash roughly using a potato masher. Mix with the other ingredients, (reserve half the breadcrumbs), stirring well.

3   Wipe the mushrooms, remove the stalks and lay the tops in a shallow ovenproof dish, black side uppermost. Chop the stalks and add to the stuffing.

4   Divide the stuffing between the mushrooms, and sprinkle the reserved breadcrumbs over the top.

QUICK BEAN SALAD

Serves 4 or 6

100g (4oz) french beans, frozen

450g (15oz) kidney beans, canned

450g (15oz) butter beans, canned

3 tablespoons salad oil

$1\frac{1}{2}$ tablespoon wine vinegar

$\frac{1}{2}$ teaspoon french mustard

Sea salt and freshly ground black pepper to taste

1 tablespoon fresh parsley, chopped

2 tomatoes

1   Thaw the french beans and cut into short lengths. Drain and rinse the kidney beans and butter beans.

2   Mix the salad oil with the vinegar, mustard, salt and pepper. Toss the beans in this dressing and pile into a salad bowl.

3   Arrange the tomatoes, cut into eighths around the edge and sprinkle the parsley in the middle.

Serves 4 as a lunch dish, 6 as a side salad.

CABBAGE BEANFEAST

Serves 4

1 small green cabbage
4 small sausages

25g (1oz) butter
100g (4oz) cooked haricot beans

1 Shred and cook the cabbage in rapidly boiling water until just tender. Drain.

2 Chop the sausages into slices and fry in the butter in a large pan until crisp.

3 Add the cabbage and the beans to the pan, toss well in the butter, put on the lid, reduce heat and cook for 2-3 minutes only.

4 Turn into a warm serving dish and serve immediately.

FRENCH BEANS WITH LETTUCE AND BACON

Serves 4

25g (1oz) butter
½ small leek, sliced
3 slices bacon, streaky

225g (8oz) french beans
   (fresh or frozen)
¼ iceberg lettuce

1 Melt the butter in a large pan, and fry the leek until soft
   but not brown. Cut the bacon into strips and fry until
   browned.

2 Top and tail the beans, and cut into short lengths. Blanch
   in boiling water for 1 minute and then drain. If using
   frozen beans allow them to thaw.

3 Add the beans to the pan and fry, stirring for 1-2 minutes.
   Shred the lettuce and stir into the beans. Cook for 30
   seconds. Turn on to a warmed serving dish and serve.

BROCCOLI WITH BLACK BEAN SAUCE

Serves 4

225g (8oz) broccoli
3 tablespoons vegetable oil
2 chilli peppers
$\frac{1}{2}$ leek
$\frac{1}{2}$ red pepper

50g (2oz) black beans,
  cooked
200ml (7 fl oz) vegetable
  stock
1 tablespoon soy sauce
1 tablespoon cornflour

1 Steam the broccoli, or cook in rapidly boiling water for
   7-8 minutes.

2 Heat the oil, fry the chopped chilli peppers, the finely
   chopped leek and red pepper until soft. Chop the beans
   and add to the sauce, stir well and cook until soft. Mix
   the stock and soy sauce and add to the pan. Cook for 1-
   2 minutes.

3   Blend the cornflour with cold water to make a paste and then add to the sauce. Cook for 1 minute.

4   Serve the sauce poured over the broccoli.

LENTILS FLORENTINE

Serves 4

100g (4oz) green lentils
225g (8oz) frozen spinach
1 clove garlic
50g (2oz) butter

150ml ($\frac{1}{4}$ pint) stock
Freshly ground black
   pepper
2 eggs

1   Wash the lentils, then cook in water for about 20-30 minutes until soft.

2   Thaw the spinach. Crush the garlic and cook in the butter until brown. Add the stock and then the spinach, season

well and cook for 20 minutes until thick. Add the cooked lentils and pour into an ovenproof dish.

3   Make a hole in the mixture for each egg, and then pour the raw eggs into the spinach and lentil sauce.

4   Cover and bake at 180°C/350°F/Gas Mark 4 for 10-15 minutes until the eggs are just set. Serve immediately.

VEGETABLE DAL
Serves 4

225g (8oz) lentils
1.2 litres (2 pints) stock
1 bay leaf
1 clove garlic
2 tablespoons vegetable oil
1 large onion
$\frac{1}{2}$ red pepper

$\frac{1}{2}$ yellow pepper
1 small cauliflower
100g (4oz) green beans
$\frac{1}{2}$ teaspoon turmeric
2 teaspoons curry powder
$\frac{1}{2}$ teaspoon coriander

1   Cook the lentils in the stock with the bay leaf added for about 20 minutes until soft.

2   Crush the garlic clove and fry in the oil until soft. Chop the onion and fry until soft. Add the thinly sliced peppers and stir well. Sprinkle in the garlic, curry powder, turmeric and coriander and cook for about 2 minutes.

3   Stir in the cauliflower florets and cook for 3-4 minutes. Roughly chop the beans and add.

4   Add the lentil mixture to the vegetables, stir well and then cook for 5 minutes, until the sauce is well combined but the vegetables remain crisp.

5   Serve hot with rice or bread

Note: Freeze for up to 3 months. Cool and pack into freezer container. Thaw for 5 hours at room temperature and reheat in an open pan, stirring occasionally.

RICE RING WITH PEAS

Serves 4

225g (8oz) long grain rice
100g (4oz) streaky bacon
1 tablespoon vegetable oil

100g (4oz) frozen french
  beans
225g (8oz) frozen peas

1 Bring a large pan of water to the boil, then tip the rice
   in and cook for 12 minutes. Rinse well in hot water. Cut
   the bacon into strips and fry in the oil until crisp.

2 Cook the beans and peas together in boiling water for
   4 minutes. Drain and cut the beans into short lengths.
   Mix with the bacon.

3 Lightly oil a ring mould (22-25cm/9-10ins in diameter),
   and press the hot rice into the mould. Invert on to a
   plate. Fill centre with mixture. Serve immediately.

STIR FRY MANGE TOUT

Serves 4

1 tablespoon vegetable oil	225g (8oz) mange tout
$\frac{1}{2}$ red pepper	100g (4oz) beansprouts
$\frac{1}{2}$ yellow pepper	2 tablespoons sherry
Small piece ginger, fresh	Few drops soy sauce
50g (2oz) cashew nuts	1 teaspoon tomato purée

1   Heat the oil in a shallow frying pan or wok. Add the thinly
    sliced peppers and the chopped ginger. Fry lightly for
    2 minutes and then stir in the cashew nuts. Stir fry until
    browned.

2   Stir in the mange tout and the beansprouts and fry,
    stirring, for 2 minutes.

3   Mix the sherry, soy sauce and tomato purée together
    and pour on top of the vegetables. Stir well and serve
    immediately.

SPANISH OMELETTE

Serves 2

½ leek
25g (1oz) butter
½ red pepper
½ green pepper
½ yellow pepper
50g (2oz) mushrooms
4 eggs

50g (2oz) mixed beans and
  peas, cooked
1 tablespoon fresh
  coriander or parsley
Sea salt and freshly ground
  black pepper.

1   Chop the leek thinly and fry in the butter. Add the peppers, thinly sliced, and stir well for 1 minute. Add the sliced mushrooms and cook until just brown.

2   Beat the eggs together with 1 tablespoon of water and season well. Pour over the vegetables in the pan. Sprinkle beans and peas on top, then turn down heat and cook for 4-5 minutes.

3   Sprinkle herbs on top and serve cut into wedges.

INDEX